You, me, and everything in between

Madison Johnson

BookLeaf Publishing

Presentation by *BookLeaf Publishing*

Web: www.bookleafpub.com

E-mail: info@bookleafpub.com

ISBN: 978-93-95890-09-0

First edition 2022

ACKNOWLEDGEMENT

To all the dreamers out there, I hope you reach the moon and beyond

To you

To all the nights spent wide awake
In the quiet, gentle night
A half empty glass of water beside my bed
The screen of my iPad illuminating my face.

To all the songs that gave me peace
A tranquil calm inside my soul
My anchor in my darkest moments
Emotions untold

To all who I ever have and will love
Know that it is pure
I wish I said it often
Instead of hiding behind my smile

To all the trees that carried me
The wind that held my secrets
Taking the weight off my shoulders
If only for a moment

To the moon and all the stars
My blanket in the night
Even when I stopped believing
You never stopped holding me

To the other part of me
Draped in shadow, hidden amongst the thicket of
leaves
I hope you know I'll find you
Even if it takes eternity

Gentle is the night

Swiftly goes the sun below the horizon
Bringing upon the sky
A swatch of blues and purples
Replacing the previous orange

The moon comes from out of hiding
The stars following suit
I wonder to myself as I watch this daily dance
Why I can't stay here forever

Ode One

4

An ode to soda
My one true love
With me through it all
Ever writing session

Out of touch

Too bright
Too loud
Skin prickling
Everything is too much

The world shifts beneath me
Floor spinning with the sky
I reach out for my headphones
Slide them over my ears

Sound slides into my body
Calming my nerves
For just a moment
Relief

Headphones

People oh people
How you work I'll never understand
In my corner I sit undisturbed
In peace

Yet you jabber on
Poking and prodding
Trying to get me to talk

Melody

There's songs in the sky
Carried by the wind
Shining in the sun
Hiding in the trees

The animals will share them
If you lend them a ear
All you have to do is listen
To the galaxy

Questioning

What is love?
A feeling in my chest?
Holding his hand,
Feeling the smile on my face?

Is it the desire for company?
Wanting to share my time with another?
Watching movies, eating popcorn
Going to eat a meal?

Or is it simply being with another?
Having someone who understands me
Enjoy me for who I am

Loved, you

Woe is me
Who fell in love with the sea
Doomed as soon as I laid my eyes
On its sparkling body

Who fell in love with the sea
With a willing smile
It's sparkling body
Swallows me whole

With a willing smile
I accept my fate
Swallowing mc whole
It washes over my head

I accept my fate
Water burns my lungs
Washing over my head
Oxygen too far gone

Water burns my lungs
My body sinks into the depths
Oxygen too far gone
I choke on salty tears

Woe is me who loved the sea
Lured by its charms
Doomed to sink to the bottom
Lifeless.

Paths

I walk along the well worn path
Covered in grassy weeds
Thorns cut at my ankles
Beads of sweat drip down my neck

Muscles ache
I want to sit down
But I continue on
To reach the end

Maze 1

A wonderful world
In this maze of mine
Infinite places
In a finite place

Critters of all sorts
Cross my path
Stopping only a moment
Before continuing on their way

Maze 2

Life is like a maze
Or so people say
But it's more like
Floating down a river

Because there is no right paths
No dead ends
No consistent smoothness
Through it all

There are bumps
Rocks
Sticks that scratch and tear
Animals that hiss and bite.

But no matter where you go
What river you travel through
You always end up
Back in the ocean

Ode 2

An ode to wizards
I envy your hats
The magic that flows through you

When I close my eyes
I like to imagine
The freedom I would have
If I were one too

Secrets

Secrets can be many things
Not just terrible things
Surprises kept from a loved one
A whisper in the dark

Thoughts that go unshared
Feelings forever alone
Carried only by the wind in the trees
And the fish in the sea

Mindful 1

Reality was made of broken glass
Cutting in my skin
Droplets of blood mixing
With the waterfall's tears

Mindful 2

Not enough
Never enough
More
More

Give your life
Your soul
For just a shred of good
A shrapnel of comfort

Mind spinning
Stubbornly pulling along
Forging my own path
As others sneer and shout

Through it all
I carry only one thing
A book, my own little world
So small, yet the harbinger of peace

Ode 3

An ode to me
But not the one here
The one across the sea
Hidden in the moon and stars

One day I'll find you
In the deep of the forest
Between the caves of the world
Then we'll be complete

Why

I dreamt of you the other day
Your face concealed in shadow
You stood facing me
Fists clenched

Your clothes were torn
Shoes worn with time
Skin roughed up
And hair a mess

And you asked me
Why

Dream

Like a fire
It starts small
Mostly smoke
Trying to hold on

Slowly it grows
I feed it more
It becomes a powerful beast
Untamable

People start to stare
Tell me I've gone to far
I stand in the ashes
Of all it's consumed

Like a fire
It gets put out
People scream
At the end I wonder

If it was worth the dream

Flavor

Cherry red
Berry blue
Lemon lime
Silly you

Purple grape
Green apple
I wish things were simple
Like flavors

www.ingramcontent.com/pod-product-compliance
Lightning Source LLC
Chambersburg PA
CBHW061327140726
47998CB00007B/2579